Islamic Empires

600–1650

Tim Leadbeater

Hodder Murray

A MEMBER OF THE HODDER HEADLINE GROUP

Acknowledgements

For my mother and father

Cover photos show a portrait of Saladin courtesy of Uffizi Gallery Florence, SEF/Art Resource, NY, and The Charge of the Cavaliers of Faramouz, from a 'Shahnama' Persian School (14th century) courtesy of the Louvre, Paris, France/Bridgeman Art Library.

The publishers would like to thank the following individuals, institutions and companies for permission to reproduce copyright illustrations in this book:

© Yann Arthus-Bertrand/ CORBIS: p3; 033446 © Bildarchiv Steffens/ Henri Stierlin, sixteenth-century Istanbul, Topkapi Library, MS Sijer I-Nebi: p4 (left); ©.Peter Sanders: p4 (right); © Dean Conger/CORBIS: p6; © CORBIS: p7; British Library, Dept of Indian and Oriental Manuscripts, Battle on Camels MS 25900: p11; © Vittoriano Rastelli/CORBIS: p14; Institut Amatller D'Art Hispànic, El Escorial (Madrid), Monastère de San Lorenzo el Real, MS S.XIII: Cántigas de Santa María: p15; Biblioteque Nationale, MS Arabe 5367 F∞/18v9: p19; © Biblioteca Apostolica Vaticana/ AR 368 10: p23; Werner Forman Archive: p25 (left and right); Nasser D. Khalili Collection of Islamic Art, CAL 242: p26 (top); © Diego Lezama Orezzoli/CORBIS: p26 (bottom); Chester Beatty MS3 folio 143r, © The Trustees of the Chester Beatty Library, Dublin: p27 (bottom); The Metropolitan Museum of Art, Rogers Fund, 1918. (17.81.4) Photograph ©1986 The Metropolitan Museum of Art: p27 (top); XYL155434 FY 1404 Takyuddin and other astronomers at the Galata observatory founded in 1557 by Sultan Suleyman, from the Sehinsahname ofx by Turkish School (16th century) University Library, Istanbul, Turkey/ Bridgeman Art Library: p28; Bodleian Library, MS Fraser 201 folio 1041r: p29 (top); Bodleian Library, MS Pococke 375 folio 3v 4r: p29 (bottom); British Library, BL MS.Or.2780f. 61r: p31; Life File Photo Library/ Mike Evans: p32; Biblioteque Nationale, MS Fr5594 folio 213: p34; Institut Amatller D'Art Hispànic, El Escorial (Madrid) Monastère de San Lorenzo el Real. MS S.XIII: Livre des Jeux de Échecs: p37; The Metropolitan Museum of Art, Francis M. Weld Fund, 1950. (50.164) Photograph ©1977 The Metropolitan Museum of Art: p39 (left); © Archivo Iconografico, S.A./CORBIS: p39; Royal Armouries, Leeds: p40; Akhbarnama, Victoria & Albert Museum, London: p41; Life File Photo Library/ Gina Green: p42; Baburnama, Victoria & Albert Museum, London: p43 (top, left); Life File Photo Library/ Barry Mayes: p43 (bottom); 1978.2597 EA, Ashmolean Museum, Oxford: p43 (top, right); British Library, BL Add Or 1039: p44.

Every effort has been made to trace and acknowledge ownership of copyright. The publishers will be glad to make suitable arrangements with any copyright holders whom it has not been possible to contact.

Artworks and Illustrations by Barking Dog Art.
Layout by Janet McCallum.

Orders: please contact Bookpoint Ltd, 130 Milton Park, Abingdon, Oxon OX14 4SB. Telephone: (44) 01235 827720. Fax: (44) 01235 400454. Lines are open from 9.00 - 6.00, Monday to Saturday, with a 24-hour message answering service. You can also order through our website www.hoddereducation.co.uk.

British Library Cataloguing in Publication Data
A catalogue record for this title is available from the British Library

ISBN-13: 978 0 340 81200 6

First Published 2004
Impression number   10 9 8 7 6 5 4
Year   2010 2009 2008 2007

Copyright © Tim Leadbeater, 2004

Printed in Italy for Hodder Murray, an imprint of Hodder Education, a member of the Hodder Headline Group, an Hachette Livre UK Company, 338 Euston Road, London NW1 3BH.

Contents

1 THE DAWN OF ISLAM

The Big Picture   2

Thinking it Through

Muhammad, the Messenger of God   4

The Qur'an and Hadith   6

Investigation

Who should succeed the Prophet?   8

2 THE EMPIRE UNFURLS 632–1000

The Big Picture   10

Thinking it Through

The conquest of Spain   12

What was Cordoba famous for?   14

Investigation

How free and mixed was Al-Andalus?   16

3 ISLAMIC CIVILISATION

The Big Picture   18

Thinking it Through

Social class   20

Investigation

The life of women   22

Thinking it Through

Cities, homes and gardens   24

Islamic arts   26

Investigation

Islamic science and technology   28

4 HOLY WARS 1000–1500

The Big Picture   30

Thinking it Through

Were the Crusades a Jihad?   32

How successful were the Crusades?   34

Investigation

Two commanders compared   36

5 NEW EMPIRES FOR OLD 1500–1650

The Big Picture   38

Thinking it Through

The Mughal Empire   40

What did the Mughals achieve?   42

Investigation

Survival skills for rulers   44

INDEX   46

THE BIG PICTURE

THIS CHAPTER ASKS

What sort of world did Islam come into?
How did Islam establish itself?
In what ways is the holy book of Islam important?
How did Islam survive the death of its founder?

THE WORLD BEFORE ISLAM

Islam took the world by surprise. It wasn't just that it spread with great speed from around 622. It was also that it came out of the Hejaz. This coastal area was part of a well-known trade route because of its important **oases** but it was far from the centres of power. So where were they at this time? Looking at a map is the best way of understanding that.

The Roman Empire had been broken up by invading tribes from Asia who established barbarian kingdoms. This forced other peoples to move on. Britain, for instance, was being settled by the Anglo-Saxons from northern Europe. These are the so-called Dark Ages of Europe.

The eastern half of the Roman Empire held together as the Byzantine Empire. The capital was Constantinople. The culture and language of the Empire became more Greek than Roman. In 622, the Emperor was Heraclius. The official religion of the Empire was Christianity in the Greek Orthodox tradition. Christian ideas had spread into Arabia.

NEW WORDS

ISLAM: (*isslarm* meaning 'submission to God' or 'peace') the new religion of the Arabs.
PAGANS: those who believe in many gods and goddesses.
OASES: places in the desert where water is available (oasis is the singular).
NOMADS: people who do not live in one settled place.
CARAVAN: a long line of camels carrying goods.
METEORITE: a rock from outer space.
KAABA: a black building, the holiest place of Islam.

SOURCE A

▲ *The Middle Eastern world c.600.*

Key
- Byzantine Empire
- Sassanian Empire
- Arabian desert
- Barbarian Kingdoms

Visigoths = Peoples or tribes

SOURCE B

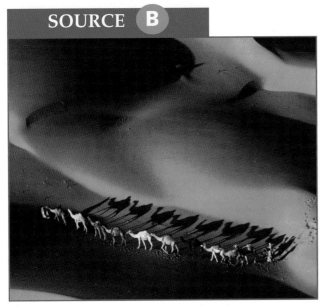

▲ A caravan moves across the desert.

The word Islam is related to the expression *asalam aleykum*, which Muslims use as a greeting like hello and means Peace be with you.

SOURCE C

A family protecting a sacred town could obtain power by making use of its religious prestige, its role in settling tribal disputes and its opportunities for trade.

▲ Albert Hourani, 1991, A History of the Arab Peoples.

THE DESERT AND THE PEOPLE

Arabia was mostly desert, as it still is today. At isolated oases in the Hejaz, there were some settled populations who farmed and traded with travellers. However, many people were **nomads** who carried goods on their **caravans** of camels along the trade routes and across the deserts. Raids by other Arabs against caravans were very common. It was a way of sharing out wealth.

The Arabs were at this time pagans. Some of their gods and goddesses were associated with particular places such as oases. These holy places would be controlled by a local tribe. One such place was Mecca where the **Kaaba**, housing a black **meteorite**, was a place of worship. It was in Mecca, in about 570, that Muhammad ibn Abdallah, the founder of Islam, was born into a powerful tribe, the Quraish.

← *The Byzantines were constantly at war with the Sassanian Empire further to the east. Its capital was at Ctesiphon and its language was Persian. In 622, the Emperor was Khosrau Parviz. The official religion, called Zoroastrianism, was about the struggle of the forces of light and darkness. The Sassanian Empire included the fertile valleys of the rivers Tigris and Euphrates. Babylon was the major centre of Jewish culture at this time.*

← *The Hejaz was part of a trading route from the Byzantine Empire through Yemen to the far east. Many Yemenis were pagans. Across the Red Sea lay Abyssinia, a Christian country ruled by a king called the Negus. Further to the east lay India and China. Further down the coast from the Hejaz was the kingdom of Yemen, a fertile area known throughout the trading world.*

Q Imagine a discussion between an experienced traveller and a young trader looking at the map. The trader is about to set off from Europe to India and wants to know about the countries he or she might pass through. The two will talk about:

- countryside
- capital
- ruler
- language
- religion
- transport
- safety and danger.

Decide whether it will be safer to go through Rome, Egypt, Hejaz and Yemen or Constantinople and Ctesiphon. Now act out their conversation.

Muhammad, the Messenger of God

Muhammad was the man who first proclaimed the religion of Islam. Muhammad is definitely not a god himself. He always said he was just the messenger of God.

MUHAMMAD'S MESSAGE

Muhammad's parents died when he was six. He was brought up by his uncle, Abu Talib, who was a powerful man in the Quraish tribe. As a young man, Muhammad made a number of trading journeys to Syria for a wealthy widow, called Khadija. She later married him and they had at least six children.

When he was in his forties (about 610), Muhammad began to spend time alone in the desert. **Muslims** believe he was visited there by the angel Gabriel who recited to him the words of **Allah**. At first, Muhammad kept this to himself but gradually told more and more people.

At this time, the Arabs believed that Allah was the chief of many gods and goddesses. However, Muhammad stated that Allah was the one and only God and the others did not exist. The Quraish began to ridicule and oppose him. They feared that Arabs would no longer come to Mecca to worship at the Kaaba.

Muslims add the phrase 'Peace and blessings be upon him' whenever they say Muhammad's name. Muhammad is often called The **Prophet**.

SOURCE A

▲ A *muezzin* on the Kaaba after it has been cleared of pagan statues.

▲ The Kaaba in modern times.

Muhammad had become the head of a collection of tribal groups that were not bound together by blood but by a shared **ideology**, an astonishing innovation in Arabian society. News of this extraordinary new supertribe spread.

▲ *Karen Armstrong, 2000,* **Islam: A Short History**

Be polite when you argue with Christians except those who do evil. Say: 'We believe in that which is revealed to us and that which is revealed to you. Our God and your God is one.'

▲ *Qur'an Surah 29:46*

In Mecca, Muhammad was a private citizen, in Medina the chief magistrate of a community. In Mecca he had to limit himself to passive opposition to the existing order, in Medina he governed. In Mecca he preached Islam, in Medina he was able to practise it.

▲ *Bernard Lewis, 1970,* **The Arabs in History**

THE HIJRA

Then both Khadija and Abu Talib died suddenly in the same year. Muhammad and his supporters, now calling themselves Muslims, came under increasing attack. Arabs in another town invited Muhammad to visit in order to settle a dispute. So he and the Muslims went to live there. This journey is so famous in Islam that it has a name – the **Hijra** – and Muslims start their calendar from that year, 622. The town was later renamed Medina, meaning the City of the Prophet.

Muhammad declared that the new One God Allah was actually the same as the old God of the Jews and Christians. At first, like them, the Muslims prayed towards the holy city of Jerusalem. Later, Muhammad revealed that the Kaaba had been built by Abraham – a figure from the Old Testament respected by Jews, Christians and Muslims. Muhammad decided that Mecca should be the holy city of Islam. Ever since, Muslims have prayed towards Mecca.

FIRST MUSLIM SUCCESSES

The Muslims defeated other tribes and their power increased. Eventually, Muhammad decided to capture Mecca in order to defeat all his Arab enemies. He was completely successful and on entering Mecca he smashed the statues of all other gods, except those of Jesus and Mary.

During Muhammad's lifetime, the Muslim Arabs conquered the rest of Arabia. Just before Muhammad's death in 632, they defeated an army of the Byzantine Empire at Tabuk. Islam was now more than a religion. It was a military force and the Muslim Arabs were on their way to becoming the rulers of their world.

1. Start a timeline of events you will read about in this book. The timeline will need to run from 600 to 1650. On one side you could have dates in the Common Era (as used in this book) and the other side could show Islamic dates starting at 0 for 622.

2. Imagine you are to interview an early Muslim for a news programme. Prepare some questions about the new religion of Islam. Your questions should cover:

■ How the religion got started

■ What's the same and what's different from before

■ How the ideas were received by Arabs

■ Changes made by Muhammad

■ How successful Islam is becoming

You might like to act out the interview.

The Qur'an and Hadith

The **Qur'an** is the holy book of Islam. According to Muslims, it contains the actual words of God as recited by the angel Gabriel to Muhammad. Muhammad could not read or write but memorised the words. It is likely that Muhammad's companions started to write down the words during his lifetime. For a while there were four different versions in circulation. About 650, Caliph Uthman (see page 8) decided on one version, which became the Qur'an known to this day.

(see page 8)

NEW WORDS

QUR'AN: (*koran*), the word means 'recitation'.
SURAH: a section of the Qur'an about a topic.
HADITH: ('traditions') stories about Muhammad's life and his explanations of Islam.
ISNAD: ('chain') the list of people who have passed on a hadith.

STRUCTURE OF THE QUR'AN

The Qur'an contains poetic advice rather than history. It is made up of **Surahs** with the longest at the beginning and the shortest at the end. The Surahs are not arranged according to an order of events or even the order in which they came to Muhammad. There is no story of Muhammad's life although certain verses are thought to refer to events in his life.

RESPECT

Muslims regard every single copy of the Qur'an as sacred. No copy of the Qur'an should be allowed to touch the floor nor should any other book be put on top of it. Muslims should wash before handling it and say special words before reading from it. The Qur'an was originally written down in Arabic and Muslims are expected to try to memorise the whole book in Arabic whatever language they actually speak.

TRADITIONAL STORIES

Writers were also collecting **hadith**. Although hadith are the words of Muhammad and not of God, they are very important in the Islamic religion. They are also important to historians because they show the beginning of a history of Islam. Hadith are introduced by an **isnad**. The Qur'an and hadith are still used by Muslims to provide guidance about how to live their lives.

SOURCE A

▲ *A Muslim reads from the Qur'an.*

In some parts of the world, old copies of the Qur'an are kept in huge caves to save them from ending up on rubbish tips or being recycled into something disrespectful.

SOURCE B

▲ *Decorated pages from the Qur'an.*

SOURCE C

According to Abu Mikhnaf who heard it from Ismail bin Yazid who heard it from Humayd bin Muslim who heard it from Jundab bin Abdallah...who heard the Prophet say.

▲ *Isnad quoted in* The History of Abu Jafar al-Tabari, *medieval Arab historian.*

AISHA

Aisha was the last and favourite wife of Muhammad. She was only 18 when he died (in her arms according to some). She lived for another 46 years.

Aisha was known for her intelligence and wisdom. She collected 2210 hadith. She is a role model for female Muslim students.

Aisha was important in establishing Islam. She even went into battle on a camel herself – some Muslims criticise this.

Aisha is sometimes called the Mother of All Believers. According to one hadith, Muhammad said to Muslims: 'You received half your religion from a woman'.

Q

1. Look at **Sources A** and **B**. What evidence do they show of ways in which Muslims show respect for copies of the Qur'an?

2. Whatever language Muslims speak in their own countries, they must learn the Qur'an in Arabic. How might this help the Arabs in holding together an empire of many different peoples?

3. Look at **Source C**. Imagine that you are collecting hadith stories about Muhammad. What facts or evidence would you be looking for to show that you could trust a particular story? In what order of importance would you put the following:

    a) A story that sounds like something in the Qur'an;

    b) A story originally told by a relative of Muhammad;

    c) A story that contains useful advice;

    d) A story that is told by more than one person.

Explain your order.

Who should succeed the Prophet?

YOUR MISSION: to investigate the murders and the power struggle after Muhammad's death.

An Arab tribe usually chose a new leader by discussion. But the Muslim community was now larger than a single family tribe. So it was going to be much harder than usual to gain complete agreement.

Many Muslims thought Ali, who was married to Muhammad's daughter Fatima, should have been **Caliph**. Others thought he was unsuitable. Let's look at the evidence.

a) Abu Bakr: I was Aisha's father and was the first Caliph even though some wanted Ali. I was old and died after two years.

b) Umar: I was originally opposed to Islam but converted, and became second Caliph. I was a successful military leader but I was killed by a prisoner of war whilst praying.

c) Ali: I was offered the Caliphate next but I refused to accept it because I disagreed with decisions taken by Abu Bakr and Umar that I would have to stick to.

d) Uthman: So I was chosen as the next Caliph. I gave too many positions of power to members of my family and became unpopular. The army became rebellious.

e) Nailah: My husband Uthman was murdered by the soldiers. I sent a message to his nephew, Muawiyya, wrapped around one of my fingers that had been cut off.

f) Ali: I was now Caliph but suspicion of my involvement in the murder of Uthman weakened my leadership. I had to go to war against fellow Muslims to get control.

g) Aisha: Riding a camel, I led an army against Ali but he captured me in battle.

h) Muawiyya: I was governor of Syria. I went into battle against Ali but it went badly. We had the idea of sticking copies of the Qur'an on our **lances** and shouting that Allah should decide the outcome of the battle through **negotiation**.

i) Ali: Some of my more religious supporters forced me to accept negotiation but this only made me and Muawiyya appear equal. Some of my supporters left my army because they believed that Allah wished the outcome to be decided in battle.

SOURCE A

How the negotiation ended.

A **shura** was organised to hear the arguments. Amr was the negotiator for Muawiyya; Abu Musa was the negotiator for Ali.

Amr let Abu Musa speak first. 'You were a companion of Muhammad and you are older. Please speak first.'

This was a trick to accustom Abu Musa to go first each time.

Abu Musa said: 'I think we should declare that these two men (Ali and Muawiyya) will allow the Muslims to choose for themselves.'

Amr said: 'I agree.'

Abu Musa went to speak to the shura and said: 'We have agreed that both of these men should stand aside and the whole community should decide the issue.'

But then Amr said: 'Abu Musa has declared his leader (Ali) is standing aside. Muawiyya will not. He has most right to become Caliph.'

Then Amr went back to Muawiyya and hailed him Caliph and Abu Musa simply left for Mecca.

▲ *From:* **The History of Abu Jafar al-Tabari,** *medieval Arab historian.*

Pictures of the faces of Muhammad and his close relatives are forbidden in Islam.

INVESTIGATION

You are the investigator!
In groups, imagine that you are in the shura listening to the arguments about whether Ali or Muawiyya should be Caliph. You must soon go back to your tribe to say which leader they should support. How will you decide? Discuss:

■ Involvement in past events such as murders and battles

■ How close the leaders are to Muhammad's family

■ How much support they have in the Muslim community

■ What the negotiators said and how they behaved.

When you have made your decision, prepare your explanation to say to the whole tribe (your class).

You will find out in the next chapter who won....

2 THE EMPIRE UNFURLS 632–1000

THE BIG PICTURE

THIS CHAPTER ASKS

Why were the Arabs so successful in creating an empire? Why did they stop?
What were the achievements of the Arabs in Spain?
How free and mixed was Muslim society in Spain?

NEW WORDS

DYNASTY: a family that holds power for several generations.
SUNNI: the main group of Muslims.
SHIAS: Muslims who believe Ali should have been Caliph.
FATIMID: named after Fatima, Muhammad's daughter who married Ali.
OPPRESSION: harsh treatment.
TYRANNY: cruel leadership.

EXPANSION

When they weren't fighting to be leader, the first four Caliphs conquered vast amounts of land from Africa to India.

CHANGE

After Ali was murdered by one of his own angry supporters, Muawiyya became Caliph. He made several changes to the way the Arab empire was controlled.

- He moved the capital to Damascus.

- He ruled more like a king who expected to be obeyed and less like an Arab chief who needed to persuade all the other chiefs.

- He arranged for his own son – Yazid – to rule after him. This was unheard of in Arab custom. This established a **dynasty** of rulers that took the family name – the Umayyads.

SOURCE A

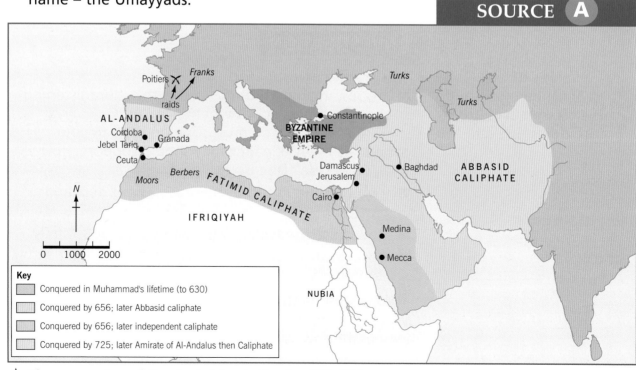

Key
- Conquered in Muhammad's lifetime (to 630)
- Conquered by 656; later Abbasid caliphate
- Conquered by 656; later independent caliphate
- Conquered by 725; later Amirate of Al-Andalus then Caliphate

▲ *The expansion of the Arab Islamic Empire 600–750.*

THE UMAYYADS

The Umayyad dynasty ruled for about 100 years and during their time the boundaries of the empire were pushed even further. Arab armies invaded Spain and were only stopped halfway through France at the battle of Poitiers in 732.

THE ABBASIDS

Eventually, another family group called the Abbasids challenged the Umayyads. People at the time called them 'the black-robed ones'. They took control in 750 by inviting the chief Umayyads to a big feast and then beating them to death. Only one escaped.

The Abbasids ruled for hundreds of years. In their time:

- They built a huge new capital at Baghdad (in modern Iraq).

- Anyone who learned Arabic and became Muslim could be successful.

- Armies made up of Arabs were replaced by a new army made up of slaves taken from the Turkish peoples of central Asia.

From this time onwards it wasn't so much an Arab Empire as an Islamic Empire.

DIVISION

Eventually, the empire began to divide. Right across the empire, there was a serious religious split between **Sunnis** and **Shias** (which lasts to this day). The north African territories broke away completely. They chose their own Caliph and a new capital at Cairo. Most of these people were Shias and they called it the **Fatimid** Empire. Spain would be the next to break away.

SOURCE B

▲ *Arab use of camels gave an advantage in long-distance campaigns.*

SOURCE C

We like your rule and justice far better than the state of **oppression** and **tyranny** under which we have been living.

▲ *Al Baladhuri, medieval historian, reporting Byzantine Christian experience of intolerance.*

SOURCE D

The Arabs who invaded the two empires were a skilled and experienced force. The prospect of land and wealth created a common interest among them; and believing God wanted them to succeed gave some of them a different kind of strength.

▲ *Albert Hourani, 1991, A History of the Arab Peoples.*

SOURCE E

The Sassanian Empire was exhausted by war with the Byzantines and had no strong leader. Byzantine resources had been stretched to their limit and they also faced barbarians from the north.

▲ *J J Saunders, 1965, A History of Medieval Islam.*

Q 1. Create a spidergram showing the reasons for the success of the Arab Muslim armies. Use different colours to show military or religious or social reasons (such as the way conquered people were treated). Use the diagram to explain why the Arab armies were so successful.

The conquest of Spain

Spain is the only country in western Europe to have been ruled by Muslims. The Islamic period was a golden age lasting over 700 years. The society was multi-racial and there were great achievements in architecture and education. During this time, Spain was called **Al-Andalus**.

NEW WORDS

AL-ANDALUS: Arabic name for Spain, meaning the place of light.
AMIR: commander.

a) 700: Spain is ruled by the Visigoths who were barbarian invaders of the Roman Empire. They are very unpopular with the Roman-Spanish farmers. The Visigoths are Christians and persecute the large Jewish population of Spain.

b) 710: The Arabs have conquered the whole of north Africa and converted the Berber tribes to Islam. The Arabs reach Ceuta, a Spanish city in north Africa ruled by a treacherous Visigoth, Duke Julian. He encourages the Arabs to invade Spain as a way of getting back at his enemies there.

c) 711: An army of 10,000 Berbers led by Tariq, a former slave, cross the 12 miles of sea between Africa and Spain. Their landing place gets called Jebel Tariq ('the Rock of Tariq') now Gibraltar.

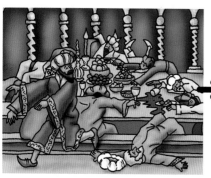

e) 750: Abd al Rahman escapes the meal-time massacre of the Umayyads by the Abbasids in Damascus (see page 11). He flees to the furthest known part of the Islamic world – Al-Andalus. He quickly establishes himself as ruler and takes the title **Amir**.

f) 929: The Umayyad dynasty of Al-Andalus has grown more and more independent of the Abbasid Caliphs in Baghdad. On 16 January 929, Abd al Rahman III declares himself Caliph of Al-Andalus.

g) 950: The Arabs have allowed a few Christian kingdoms to survive in the north of Spain. The Caliphate breaks up. The Christians begin to fight back.

The Arabic phrase *amir al bahr*, commander of the sea, was borrowed into English as admiral.

d) 712: Tariq's success encourages his Arab ruler Musa to come with a larger army. Within ten years, the whole of Spain has been conquered and renamed Al-Andalus. Musa's son has married King Roderick's widow – the first of many Muslim-Christian marriages for political purposes.

SOURCE A

Once Roderick was killed, no other kings remained in Spain. Duke Theodomir surrendered on the following terms: the Muslims were not to harm him, his people or their churches. In return he and his people would not harm the Muslims or help their enemies and they would pay the Muslims an annual tribute.

▲ *Derek Lomax, 1978,* **The Reconquest of Spain.**

SOURCE B

The Christians praised the tolerance and justice of the conquerors and preferred their rule to that of the Visigoths and Franks.

▲ *Reinhart Dozy, 1972,* **Spanish Islam.**

SOURCE C

Europe seemed remarkably unattractive to the Muslims – there were few opportunities for trade in that primitive backwater, little booty to be had and the climate was terrible.

▲ *Karen Armstrong, 2000,* **Islam: A Short History.**

SOURCE D

What really put a stop to the Arab advance in Europe was a great Berber revolt against Arabs taking the best farmland.

▲ *J J Saunders, 1965,* **A History of Medieval Islam.**

h) 1086: A new wave of Muslims from north Africa take over. These people are known as Moors and Al-Andalus is sometimes referred to as Moorish Spain.

i) 1340: Spanish Christians reconquer most of Spain. The Moors are allowed to rule the Kingdom of Granada. In 1492, the Christians finally expel all Muslims and Jews from Spain. The age of tolerance is over.

Q **1.** From the cartoon strip and **Sources A** and **B**, identify three reasons why the Arabs did not encounter much resistance in their conquest of Spain.

2. Look at **Sources C** and **D**. Why did the Arabs not try harder to conquer Europe after their defeat at Poitiers in 732? What might have happened if they had?

What was Cordoba famous for?

The capital of Al-Andalus at Cordoba rivalled Baghdad for its size, architecture and culture. Contemporary reports speak of thousands of bookshops and bathhouses. The city had running water, at the time a considerable engineering feat. Widespread **irrigation** created fertile farmland all around.

NEW PALACE

Caliph Abd al Rahman III built a palace – the Madinat al Zahra – on a hill overlooking a river outside Cordoba. It was really a small town for those running the Caliphate. The offices were arranged up the hillside according to status. There were embassies of European kingdoms. When **ambassadors** came they first had to walk along a three-mile line of soldiers. They then met officials in ever grander rooms. Finally they were shown into the room of the Caliph only to find him sitting in simple clothes reading a book.

BOOKS AND WRITING

His successor Al-Hakim created a library of 40,000 books. These included the only available translations of ancient Greek books. **Scholars** came to study them from all over Europe. Al-Andalus was also famous for its poets and musicians – the film stars of their day.

Muslim poets in Al-Andalus developed a new form of poetry. There were separate short verses each with the same set of rhymes. If this sounds very like European poetry, that's because it is. Modern European poetry took shape in southern France at the time when the Moorish **culture** in Spain was at its height. Some believe that the French poets borrowed the new style from the Moors.

Muslims created stories by putting together a string of adventures by a hero. These too were popular in Spain where the first European novels – such as Don Quixote – would be written shortly after using that same structure.

NEW WORDS

IRRIGATION: a large system of ditches to carry water to fields.
SCHOLAR: someone who studies in great detail.
CULTURE: artistic activities and education.
AMBASSADOR: an official visitor from another country.

SOURCE A

The Great Mosque of Cordoba. The Arabs copied the horseshoe arch of the Visigoths, putting it on top of short pillars from Roman ruins to create a distinctive architectural style.

FASHION

The image of the Cordoban court was one of wealth, luxury and easy living. Arab nobles drank from elegant glass goblets rather than the heavy metal ones used in Europe. They ate fancy new vegetables such as asparagus and artichoke. Cordoba became a centre of new fashions. At one point, it was the height of cool for young men to paint their legs gold.

SOURCE B

▲ *Moorish and Christian musicians playing the lute together from a thirteenth-century Book of Chants.*

ZIRYAB

Ziryab was a famous singer and guitar player in Baghdad. He had to leave because his music teacher became jealous of his success. He came to Cordoba in 822. The Amir was so impressed he paid Ziryab a salary. Ziryab had a huge influence on the style of living. We still follow some of his ideas today.

Among the things Ziryab introduced were:

- a fixed order of courses in a meal
- different styles of clothes in different seasons
- hairdressing and dying beards with henna
- using perfume on bodies and in houses
- cleaning teeth with sweet-smelling paste.

SOURCE C

All the young Christians know only the language and books of the Arabs, building up great libraries of them at enormous cost and loudly proclaiming everywhere that this literature is worthy of admiration. They compose poetry in Arabic with greater art than the Arabs themselves.

▲ *The complaint of Alvaro of Cordoba about 850.*

The word guitar comes from an Arabic word.

SOURCE D

No place in the Islamic lands can match the size of its population, the area of its markets, cleanliness of its inhabitants, construction of its mosques and number of its baths and hostelries.

▲ *Ibn Hawkal, medieval geographer.*

Q

1. Explain in your own words how important the culture of Al-Andalus was in spreading ideas into Europe.

2. Imagine you are a poet looking for a job at the court of Abd al Rahman. Make a list of the things you ought to include in a poem praising what you have seen of the culture of Al-Andalus. Compose a short poem and recite it to a neighbour.

How free and mixed was Al-Andalus?

YOUR MISSION: to discover how free and mixed people and religion were in Al-Andalus.

These slaves (1) have been brought from the edges of the Islamic Empire. Some have been captured in battle, others have been bought simply to be sold again. Male black slaves from Nubia and Ifriqiyah worked in homes; male white slaves from Eastern Europe were for the army; female slaves were often dancers and singers in the houses of Arab nobles. They just speak their own different languages at the moment.

There were 14,000 slaves in Al-Andalus. Slavery existed long before Islam. It was well regulated. Slaves were entitled to medical attention and care in old age. It was forbidden to make slaves of Muslims. Slaves who converted to Islam might be freed.

This noble (2) comes from one of the Arab families who led the invasion of Spain. His family were given good farmland in reward. He gets a salary for advising the Amir. He does not pay taxes. He is buying slaves to sell on his travels. He speaks Arabic.

These are peasant farmers of the original **Iberian** ethnic group (9). They have come to sell food. They might well speak Spanish-Latin mixed with ancient Iberian words.

This Visigothic Christian soldier is a **mercenary** (10). His family land was given to Arabs after the invasion. He is adopting Arab dress and customs and is known as a **mozarab**. He speaks Spanish-Latin and a bit of Arabic.

This Jewish money-changer (11) and Frankish Christian slave trader (8) are known as People of the Book (The Old Testament of the Bible). They are free to follow their own religions. However, they must not criticise Islam in public, may not carry weapons nor marry Muslims. They should wear yellow items of clothing to show they are not Muslims. They can become wealthy. They have to pay taxes – but not more than they can afford. This is also to discourage them from converting to Islam because then they would not have to pay taxes and the Amirate would get less money.

Across Europe in the Middle Ages, Jewish money-lenders did what banks do today. There was a golden age of Jewish culture in Al-Andalus and many Christians were promoted to high positions in the service of the Amir. Jews speak Hebrew and Arabic. Franks speak French-Latin.

NEW WORDS

IBERIAN: the original people of Spain.
MERCENARY: a soldier who fights for anyone who pays.
MOZARAB: 'an almost Arab'.

ABD AL RAHMAN III
The Arab Caliph Abd al Rahman III is all mixed up himself. His grandmother is an Iberian princess and his mother an Iberian slave-wife. As a result he has fair skin and a reddish beard, which he dyes black to make himself look more like an Arab.

This Berber soldier (3) is a convert to Islam and has been adopted by an Arab family. He is angry that he has only been given poor farmland dangerously near the border with the Christian kingdoms. He pays more taxes than the Arab nobles do. He speaks a north African language and a bit of Arabic.

This is a Muslim judge (4) accompanied by a Jewish market inspector (5) from the palace. They speak in Arabic.

This Christian prince from the Basque province (6) has brought his daughter in order to arrange a marriage with an Arab noble. As Christians, no matter how royal, they are not allowed to ride horses in Islamic territory. They speak Basque and Arabic.

This woman poet (7) has just arrived from Baghdad. She is actually an agent from the Abbasid court spying on the Umayyad dynasty in Al-Andalus. She speaks Arabic.

INVESTIGATION

You are the investigator!
You are a scholar from Northern Europe who has come to visit the famous library at Cordoba. Your job is to write to your fellow scholars back in England about what you have seen in Al-Andalus. You should mention:

- different ethnic groups and languages
- freedom of religion
- architecture
- books and poetry
- food and fashion.

There is to be no compulsion in religion.
Qur'an Surah 2 the Cow, v 256.

THE BIG PICTURE

THIS CHAPTER ASKS

Which aspects of life bound the empire together?
How were societies and cities organised?
What was life like for women?
What were the achievements of artists and scientists?

NEW WORDS

CONSENSUS: widespread informal agreement by discussion.
ANALOGIES: similar situations or explanations.
ADULTERY: having sex with someone not your husband or wife.
MINARET: tall thin tower.
IMAM: a religious teacher.

All Muslims still feel like brothers and sisters in one big international family. Their name for the group of Islamic countries is The House of Peace (although there are sometimes arguments, of course, as in many family houses). What would a medieval Arab travelling from Spain to India have recognised as familiar features of life and the law?

The Arabic word *sharia* means 'the way to the watering hole'.

THE GOOD LIFE

Islam isn't just about personal faith. It is also very concerned with social justice and public behaviour. Islamic law is known as Sharia. It has four roots:

■ statements in the Qur'an

■ traditions of judgments going back to decisions made by Muhammad

■ the **consensus** of the Muslim people

■ **analogies**.

Sharia doesn't just state what it is wrong to do. It also sets out what good behaviour consists of. There are five categories of conduct:

■ obligatory, e.g. praying

■ recommended, e.g. giving slaves freedom

■ permitted, e.g. becoming wealthy

■ discouraged, e.g. divorce

■ prohibited, e.g. drinking wine, eating pork.

Sharia, like other medieval codes of law, has fairly brutal punishments, such as cutting hands off thieves and executing people for a range of crimes, including **adultery**.

MOSQUES

What would a traveller to a new city expect to find in a mosque? A muezzin would chant *Allahu Akhbar* (God is Great) from the top of the **minaret** to call people to prayer. There would be a large courtyard with washing facilities and a place to leave shoes. Inside there would be prayer mats and fantastic wall decoration – intricate patterns or writings from the Qur'an but no statues or pictures. Those praying would form long lines facing towards Mecca, touching their foreheads to the ground. They would then listen to a talk from an **imam** standing on a set of steps. There would be a separate area for women to pray. Most of these things can be found in any mosque today.

SOURCE A

▲ *An imam talks to Muslims in a mosque.*

THE FIVE PILLARS OF ISLAM

The five pillars are actually activities that build a civilised Islamic society. The pillars are strong because every Muslim is expected to do them. The five pillars are:

1. Believing in the one God and Muhammad as his messenger.

2. Praying five times a day.

3. Giving money to the poor.

4. Fasting in the holy month of Ramadan.

5. Pilgrimage to Mecca once in a lifetime.

Q

1. Why do you think the word Sharia is used to describe law and good behaviour?

2. Work out an analogy: Drinking wine is prohibited in the Qur'an. How have lawyers decided that beer – which is not mentioned – should also be prohibited?

3. Discuss what five pillars of modern European life might be. Design a poster to explain the five pillars of Islam and the five pillars of European culture.

Social class

Muslims might say they were brothers and sisters sharing the same ideas but that didn't mean they were equal in power or respect. Within the empire, there were various classes. These included a large middle class hundreds of years before its appearance in Europe.

THE CALIPH

At the top of society was the ruler – the Caliph. The Caliphs who succeeded Muhammad were expected to be leaders in peace, in battle and in religious matters. The Abbasid Caliph was addressed as The Shadow of God on Earth.

The Caliph would always appear in public with two people. First, his **vizier** and second the public executioner with his huge axe. This was to remind people of the Caliph's power over life and death.

In later times, the Caliph was a more symbolic figure and the real military power was in the hands of the **sultan**, or rather the sultans of different regions.

NEW WORDS

VIZIER: the chief adviser to the Caliph.
SULTAN: the military commander, later a local ruler.
LUNAR CALENDAR: all months exactly 28 days.
WARRAQEEN: book copiers and sellers.
SHEIKH: tribe leader chosen by family elders.

Other powerful groups were the judges who were highly educated in religious law, and of course the army. Increasingly this was made up of highly trained slaves from central Asia.

PEASANTS AND WORKERS

At the bottom of society were the peasants who worked on farms (often owned by city-dwellers) or herded animals around. Although uneducated, the peasants actually had to use two calendars – a solar calendar for farming and the Islamic **lunar calendar**, which is out of step with the solar calendar.

SOURCE **A**

▲ *Classes in the Islamic Empire. Can you spot the caliph, the vizier, the executioner, traders and soldiers?*

In between, there were various groups within a relatively large middle class. The wealthiest were the merchants, especially those who traded in goods over long distances. Then there were craftspeople and shopkeepers, market inspectors, tax collectors and office workers in the palace.

One particular group was the **warraqeen**. They made paper, copied manuscripts, bound them into books and sold them. Some books were thousands of pages long. The shops were also meeting places for scholars who might come to listen to a new book being dictated and copied down.

Within these classes, there were other ways in which people grouped themselves. The most important was the family, usually of three generations, living in the same house. Families were part of a tribe, led by a **sheikh**. In a city, related tribes or ethnic groups would build houses near each other. These sections of the city were known as quarters, each with its own name.

SOURCE B

Religious and royal authority are united in the caliph so that he can devote the available strength to both of them at the same time.

▲ *Ibn Khaldun, medieval historian.*

SOURCE C

The trust in good rulers able to resist temptation meant that there was no development of a social balance of power such as a parliament provides.

▲ *Olivier Roy, 1994,* **The Failure of Political Islam.**

Before 900, a Muslim scholar, Al-Yaqubi, counted more than 100 bookshops in just one part of Baghdad.

Q

1. Look at **Source B**. Explain why the writer thinks the Caliph should have all the power. Look at **Source C**. What does this writer suggest could go wrong with this situation? How might the times when they are writing explain their different views?

2. Draw a pyramid-shaped diagram using drawings and labels to show the different classes of people in the Islamic Empire.

The life of women

YOUR MISSION: to provide advice about the situation of women in medieval Islam.

Some modern westerners think women have been treated rather badly in Islamic societies. How true was this in the medieval empire? Let's consider the evidence.

LAW

The Qur'an says that men and women are basically equal in the eyes of Allah. However, the Qur'an and Sharia based on hadith set out unequal rights in law and human affairs. A daughter can only inherit half the amount given to a son. A man may divorce a woman by simply saying so three times whereas a woman must persuade a judge.

NEW WORDS

PATRIARCHY: a society controlled by men for the benefit of men.
HIJAB: a headscarf or veil.
BURKA: a loose garment to cover the whole head and body, with holes to see through.
DOWRY: a large sum of money provided by the woman's family when marriage takes place.
PURDAH: custom of keeping noble women behind a curtain at public events.

SOURCE A

A man is allowed up to four wives if he can treat them all fairly.

▲ *Quran, Surah 4.3: The Women.*

HONOUR AND RESPECT

The position of women in Islamic culture was partly a result of **patriarchal** ideas about tribal honour. Women were respected, as the mothers of sons in particular, but their freedom was controlled in order to preserve their honour and therefore the family's. Islamic writers regarded European sexual behaviour as strange and careless.

SOURCE B

It is patriarchy and not the Qur'an which requires women to cover their faces with the **hijab** or in very Islamic countries cover their whole bodies with the **burka**.

▲ *Malise Ruthven, 1997,* Islam.

WORK AND MEETING PEOPLE

SOURCE C

Most women were engaged in some kind of work. The hijab was not for the poor. Women were shopkeepers and craft workers, particularly in the making of rugs and carpets, the main industry of the medieval Muslim world.

▲ *Gavin Hambly, 1998,* Women in the Medieval Islamic World.

SOURCE D

Some women got money through inheritance, others as a dowry and some actually seem to have participated in trade perhaps on the model of the Prophet's wife Khadija.

▲ *Ronald Jennings, 1998,* Women in the Medieval Islamic World.

SOURCE E

Women from richer households met each other on visits, at marriages and births, and at public bath houses on women only days.

▲ *Albert Hourani, 1991,* A History of the Arab Peoples.

SOURCE F

▲ *Noblewomen in a garden listening to Bayad, a popular singer and luteplayer.*

SEX

Islam has a very realistic attitude to sex. Sex is recognised as a pleasure not just the means of making babies. A Persian book, *The Perfumed Garden,* has been a famous sex-manual for Europeans since 1500. Warriors who die in battle are promised that there will be 72 virgins waiting for them when they arrive in heaven.

SOURCE G

Muhammad had sex with nine wives in one night.

▲ *Hadith attributed to Al-Bukhari.*

SOURCE H

Sex is an example of the delights in Paradise because it would not work to make a promise of delights people have not experienced.

▲ *Al Ghazali, medieval Muslim philosopher.*

SULTAN RADIYYA BINT ILTUTMISH

Radiyya was the favourite child of the Sultan of Delhi. When her father died, her mother tried to kill her. Radiyya went out onto a palace balcony and made a speech to the crowd. The people rose up in revolt and made her Sultan.

In her short reign, Radiyya:

- Won battles and conquered more land in India

- Wore men's clothing and rode elephants

- Refused to stay in **purdah**

- Had a love affair with an African slave who was then murdered

- Was imprisoned but married the man who captured her.

INVESTIGATION

You are the investigator!

Imagine you write an advice column in a medieval magazine. You have received a letter from a European princess whose father is considering arranging a marriage to a sultan. She wants to know what to expect and whether she should agree to it. Write your reply to be published in the magazine. You should explain what she could expect about:

- legal and religious attitudes
- what different women were free to do
- issues of honour and respect
- attitudes to love and sex.

You should conclude with your overall advice about what she should do.

Cities, homes and gardens

Medieval Islamic cities were the largest in the world. Baghdad may have had nearly a million inhabitants with Cairo and Cordoba not far behind. It would be hundreds of years before London grew to that size. Trade flourished between many more smaller cities. News, intrigue and all kinds of artistic, scientific and religious ideas got passed on as well.

A trader or traveller arriving at an Islamic city would have recognised familiar features wherever they were in the empire. These include:

- On the outskirts, market gardens, **caravanserais**, and factories and smelly industries such as **tanneries**.

- Inside the city, families and tribes would have houses near each other in a particular quarter. Types of shops or workers, such as carpet-makers, might be grouped together.

- At the centre would be the **madina** and the central mosque. Nearby would be the **souk** or **bazaar** and warehouses. There would be hospitals and **madrassas**.

- Any royal palace, offices and barracks might be just outside the city for security. Baghdad was only a village when the capital of the empire was moved there. A whole new city was planned and built with a circular **citadel** in the centre containing all the palaces and barracks.

- Protection of health and the environment. Certain areas had to be left without buildings. Water for the city was taken out of rivers upstream; sewage was flushed out downstream.

HOW WERE HOUSES DESIGNED?

Houses were built for privacy not showing off. The outer walls had screened windows and the main door was very plain. Even when the door was open, a wall inside blocked the view into the house.

➤ *A typical house in a Muslim city.*

NEW WORDS

CARAVANSERAI: a place where camel trains would stop for food and water – a bit like a motel today.
TANNERY: a place where animal skins are cleaned for making into leather.
MADINA: central open place.
SOUK/BAZAAR: a market building.
MADRASSA: a school.
HAREM: a place reserved for women in a house or palace.
CITADEL: a fortified part inside a city.

SOURCE A

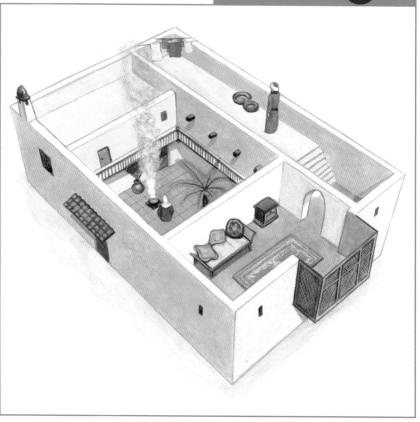

SOURCE B

▲ *The interior of the bazaar at Isfahan, Iran, which has been operating since 200.*

SOURCE C

▲ *Muslims loved gardens within their homes and palaces. Heaven was imagined as a garden. The richest would have gardens with running water and fountains.*

The rooms would face into a central courtyard where all the cooking was done. Houses could be three storeys high with balconies overlooking the courtyard. Every dwelling, whether a house or a palace, had a **harem**. There was little furniture but a great many furnishings – carpets, rugs, cushions and curtains.

The Arabic phrase *dar as sina*, became *arzenale* in Italian and then arsenal in English. It meant workshop or factory but now means a weapons store.

SOURCE D

There was a close but difficult relationship between the two centres of activity in any city – the palace and the market. They needed each other but they wanted different things.

▲ *Albert Hourani, 1991,* A History of the Arab Peoples.

Q

1. Why was water in a garden a sign of wealth? Explain why wealthy people at this time might want to keep their houses private.

2. Look at **Source D**. Make two lists: one of things the traders might want a city to be like; one of the things the ruler would like.

3. Draw a plan of how you think Baghdad was laid out. Think about a town or city where you live. Can you identify different areas for different purposes?

Islamic arts

Muslims respect skill with words. The Arabs had always loved reciting poetry. The Qur'an also had to be memorised and recited. Any attempt to imitate the style of the Qur'an was strictly forbidden. However, poets created new styles and daring new subjects. There were love stories and a type of poem celebrating getting drunk and having a good time which is definitely un-Islamic!

SOURCE A

▲ *The art of calligraphy combines the arts of words, handwriting and design in imaginative ways.*

NEW WORDS

DERVISH: a dancing Sufi.
SECULAR: to do with everyday life or without a religious purpose.

Carpet weavers would always put a fault in the pattern to remind everyone that human beings cannot be perfect.

SOURCE B

ART

Officially, in Islamic culture, any portrayal of human beings or animals was regarded as offensive because it suggested an imitation of Allah's own creations. As a result, artists concentrated on fantastically intricate geometric and floral patterns for decorating mosques, carpets and books. Human sculpture is completely missing.

◄ *Safavid Dome (see page 38): Mosques were often covered with amazing patterns and the words of the Qur'an.*

WHY DID WHIRLING DERVISHES WHIRL?

The situation of music and dance in Islam is complicated. Officially, they are frowned on because they seem frivolous and seem to lead to drinking alcohol. But pictures, music textbooks and historical accounts show that music and dance were a regular part of **secular** life and palace events.

Not only that, music is closely involved in religious activity. The Qur'an may be chanted on special occasions and the call of the muezzins from the minarets is musical rather than shouted.

Muslims of the Sufi tradition try to get closer to God by putting themselves in a trance-like state. The whirling **Dervishes** do this by circling round on one leg. Although they don't dance very fast, the effect is heightened by the long, flared coats they wear.

SOURCE C

▲ *The Whirling Dervishes from a Persian manuscript of 1490.*

◄ *Mughal feast to celebrate birth of Jahangir (see page 41) painted 1600.*

SOURCE D

Q

1. Look at **Source B**. Identify Arabic lettering, floral and geometric decoration on the dome. Try to copy a little of each one.

2. Compare **Sources C** and **D**. What is different about the dancers and what they are wearing? What might this evidence in the pictures suggest about why Islam tolerated the Sufi dervishes but disapproved of secular music and dance?

3. Try your hand at designing a calligraphic animal or building in English. Use **Source A** to give you ideas.

Islamic science and technology

YOUR MISSION: to research Islamic scientific achievements for a TV documentary.

Medieval Muslims translated ancient scientific books and made many discoveries and inventions themselves. Modern western civilisation got started because this work was passed on to Europe through Al-Andalus/Spain.

Here are ten of their top achievements:

1. The greatest feat of the mathematician Al-Khwarizmi (d.850) was literally *nothing*! He knew the old Roman number system could not be used easily for mathematics because it used letters, e.g. M = 1000, C = 100. So he improved the Indian number system which shows size by rules for the position of the numerals, e.g. 1000 is 10 times bigger than 100. Al-Khwarizmi's system also developed the zero (an Arabic word) which was an unknown concept for the Romans. The zero makes possible **binary code**. So we could say that Al-Khwarizmi's mathematics textbooks have led to space travel and the internet.

2. Al-Battani (d.929) calculated the **circumference** of the earth and the exact length of the year to within 24 seconds.

3. Al-Fazari (d.790) developed the astrolabe into a kind of handheld computer for working out where you are in the world from the position of the stars. This device greatly speeded up world exploration.

4. Al-Haytham (d.1039) proposed that we see by receiving light bouncing off other objects rather than our eyes shooting out light beams themselves!

5. Although they didn't invent them, Muslim chemists were the first to make and sell paint, soap, glass, ink and paper in large quantities. The word chemistry comes from an Arabic word.

6. Muslim technologists spread the use of waterwheels, which would become the first energy source of the European industrial revolution.

7. Muslim medicine made great advances. Baghdad alone had 60 hospitals, with

SOURCE A

Roman numerals	Arabic numerals	Modern European numerals
	٠	0
I	١	1
II	٢	2
III	٣	3
IV	٤	4
V	٥	5
VI	٦	6
VII	٧	7
VIII	٨	8
IX	٩	9
X	١٠	10

SOURCE B

▲ *An Islamic observatory. The man at the back is pointing to the astrolabe he is holding.*

separate wards for men and women, at a time when there were probably none in the whole of Europe. Doctors were properly trained and understood how infections are passed on. Ibn Sina (d.1037) wrote a medical textbook that was used in Europe for 700 years. Ibn Nafis (d.1288) discovered that the blood circulates around the body 400 years before Europeans claimed to discover it.

8. Muslim mariners popularised the lateen sail. Previously, square-rigged sails meant boats could only travel in the direction of the wind. The lateen sail – adjustable so it could even go pointing forwards – enables boats to navigate and zig-zag forward whatever the wind direction. The combination of both sails made possible the European conquest of the Americas.

9. Muslim geographers made maps of the whole world known to them. Before this, Europeans thought that Islam covered the whole globe apart from Europe. Knowing about India, Asia and China led to European exploration and empires.

10. Muslims created the first university in the world – the Al-Azhar in Cairo, established in 970.

SOURCE C

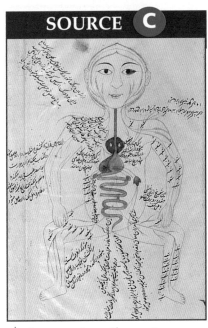

▲ *A seventeenth-century Persian diagram showing blood vessels and internal organs.*

SOURCE D

▲ *A twelfth-century map of the Islamic world by Al-Idrisi. Arabia is in the centre and Europe in the bottom right corner.*

INVESTIGATION

You are the investigator!

You are a researcher for the modern Arab satellite television station Al-Jazeera. You are making a documentary for primary school children about Islamic scientific achievements. You must write the script. You should mention:

■ inventions and discoveries

■ developments of older ideas

■ things that were later used in Europe

■ other results or effects of Islamic achievements.

When you have written the script, you could find photos or illustrations to go with the words. If you have access to a video camera, you could video the pictures whilst speaking your script into the microphone. Don't forget to make a title picture for the start and a list of credits to show who helped to make it at the end.

THIS CHAPTER ASKS

Which were the most significant of the invasions of the Islamic Empire?
How important was religion as a factor in the invasions?
How do the two most admired leaders of their age compare?

NEW WORDS

CRUSADE: from the French word for cross, an attack by Christians.
STEPPE: open grassland extending hundreds of miles.
OUTREMER: over the sea.

WAVES OF INVASIONS

By 1000, the power of the Abbasid Caliphs in Baghdad was hollow. The empire was not well organised even though it was still getting larger. Many parts were ruled by local Sultans. There was disagreement and conflict between them. These divisions left the empire vulnerable to outside attacks. In this middle period of the Islamic Empire there were four waves of invasions.

THE TURKS

First to come were the Turks from central Asia. They were looking for new territory but were blocked by the strength of the Chinese Empire further to the east. Some

Turks had already been invited by the Caliphs to form an elite unit of the Islamic army. From 1040, whole armies of Turkish cavalry moved through the Islamic Empire and seized the capital Baghdad in 1055. They allowed the Caliph to remain in place but Turkish nobles took all the positions of power in the central part of the empire. They allowed the edges of the empire to break away.

THE RECONQUEST OF SPAIN

In Al-Andalus after 1000, the caliphate broke down into several weaker Arab kingdoms. This gave the Christian armies the chance to reconquer from the north. Over in Africa,

SOURCE A

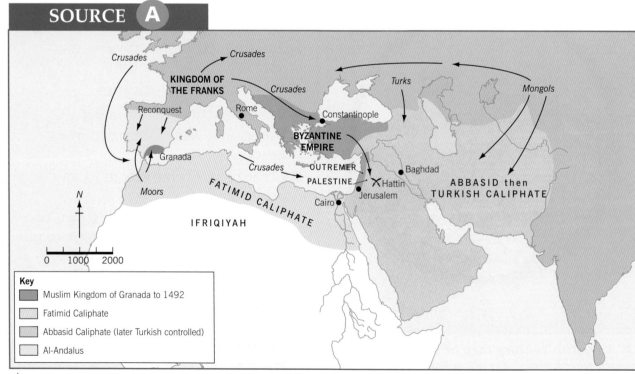

Key
- Muslim Kingdom of Granada to 1492
- Fatimid Caliphate
- Abbasid Caliphate (later Turkish controlled)
- Al-Andalus

▲ *Attacks on the Islamic Empire 1000–1500.*

THE BIG PICTURE

➤ *Mongol warlord Genghis Khan shown speaking in a mosque in a painting from 1387. The picture is designed to suggest God had encouraged him to conquer the Muslims.*

there was a new and strongly religious Berber Empire. The Muslims of Al-Andalus believed that the Christian success might be a result of their own religious weakness so in 1091 they invited the Berbers to fight with them. The Berbers (or Moors) promptly established themselves as the new rulers. They slowed down the Christian advance. The small kingdom of Granada clung on until 1492 when both Moors and Jews were thrown out of Spain.

THE CRUSADES

Meanwhile, by 1100 the Turkish armies had pushed on into Anatolia and threatened Constantinople, capital of the Byzantine Empire. The Byzantine emperor appealed for help. In response, between 1096 and 1300, at least eight **Crusades** from western Europe set off to attack Muslims – but in Palestine not Anatolia. They established a group of Christian colonies on the coast, known as **Outremer**, which lasted until 1291. The Turks finally captured Constantinople in 1453.

THE MONGOLS

The last invasion was the most devastating. The Mongols were nomadic tribes from the **steppes** in the heart of Asia. From 1206, they united under the warlord Genghis Khan. In order to maintain this new unity, he looked for new lands to conquer. Christian ambassadors encouraged him to attack the Muslims. He died before he could finish the job but his grandson, Hulagu, invaded the Islamic Empire in 1255. In 1258, the Mongols captured Baghdad and massacred 800,000 people. The streets were full of stinking bodies. They even killed all the cats and dogs.

The Mongols thought it unlucky to execute a ruler with a sword inside his own city. So they rolled the Caliph up in a carpet and trampled him to death with their heaviest horses.

Q

1. Draw a spidergram to show the Islamic Empire and each of the four invasions. For each invasion show a cause and a consequence. Use different colours to show the different causes such as religion or the wish to seize more land. Which of the invading forces were strongly religious? Were they the most successful?

2. Create a newspaper front page reporting on the waves of invasions. You should have a separate article for each invasion with a headline and story. The most important invasion (in your opinion) should have the biggest headline and story, be at the top and perhaps be illustrated. Then work down the page.

Were the Crusades a Jihad?

The word **jihad** strikes fear in the West. In Europe (and America now) jihad is thought to be the threat of a never-ending holy war to conquer more land and destroy Christianity. Certainly, the huge success of the early Islamic Empire looked like that. But were the Crusades the same only the other way round?

WHAT STARTED THE CRUSADES OFF?

We have seen that the Crusades started after an appeal for military help from the Byzantine Emperor, Alexius. However, when **Pope** Urban II urged the Franks to respond, he made the message more religious in two ways. First, the Pope promised that anyone who died during a crusade would definitely go to heaven. Second, the objective changed from helping the Byzantines to capturing Jerusalem.

WHY IS JERUSALEM SO IMPORTANT?

Jerusalem is a sacred city for Jews, Christians and Muslims. Jerusalem had been in Muslim control since 638, some 450 years before the Crusades started. Christian pilgrimages had been allowed into the city until 1071, 16 years after the Turks took control.

NEW WORDS

JIHAD: ('struggle') the struggle of each Muslim to be good and struggle against other people's lack of belief.
POPE: the supreme head of the Catholic tradition of Christianity.
HERETIC: someone who follows a breakaway religious idea.
PRINCIPALITY: land ruled by a prince.

Some of the crusaders were fighting monks. One such group was the Knights of St John. They are known today as the St John's Ambulance Association, and assist at football matches and public events.

SOURCE A

▲ *The Old City area of Jerusalem today: In the foreground is the wall of Solomon's temple of the ancient Jews; above it is the golden Dome of the Rock mosque, site of Muhammad's Night Flight; not far away is the dome of the Church of the Holy Sepulchre marking the place where Jesus rose from the dead.*

SOURCE B

The Crusades were an experiment in overseas conquest motivated by money with religion as a boost. The significant figures were European traders, warlike and ambitious barons, younger sons in search of **principalities** and sinners in search of profitable forgiveness.

▲ *Bernard Lewis, 1970,* The Arabs in History.

WERE THERE OTHER REASONS FOR THE CRUSADES?

Between 1095 and 1295, thousands of Europeans 'took the Cross'. This meant that they promised to travel thousands of miles to invade Palestine and liberate, that is to capture, the Holy City. But historians have said that it wasn't just religion that made them enthusiastic. Other reasons include:

■ new lands to conquer and own

■ opportunities to get rich through plunder

■ opening new trade routes to the East

■ respect gained by successful warriors.

The Second Crusade set off even though Jerusalem was in Christian hands. They simply wanted to get back part of Outremer recaptured by the Muslims. Later, Crusades were made against pagans and **heretics** in Europe.

THE CHILDREN'S CRUSADE

The craziest Crusade was the Children's Crusade in 1212. The idea was that God – the Christian God – would make sure the holiest, purest people succeeded where others had failed. Children had to be purer than adults because they had not lived long enough to become bad. So thousands of children formed a Crusade, walking through France towards the Mediterranean ports. By the time they got there, most of the children were exhausted, quickly got sick and died before they could even set sail for Palestine.

SOURCE C

The lands you are travelling to are much richer and more fertile; many of you will find a more prosperous way of life there.

▲ *Abbot Martin of Paris, 1201.*

SOURCE D

Soldier, you now have a cause for which you can fight without endangering your soul. If you are a merchant, do not miss this opportunity of a splendid bargain.

▲ *St Bernard of Clairvaux, 1146.*

SOURCE E

They would not have travelled so far to fight in armour in such heat unless they had strong religious feelings.

▲ *Carole Hillenbrand, 2003, discussion on BBC Radio 3.*

SOURCE F

The crusaders were simply called Franks, whether they came from Sicily, Hungary or Scotland. No Arabic word was coined to indicate that these intruders were engaged in a religious form of warfare.

▲ *Richard Fletcher, 2003,* The Cross and the Crescent. *An Arabic word for the Crusades was only created in the nineteenth century, 750 years later.*

Q

1. Make a table to show the different groups of people who joined Crusades. Then complete the rest of it:

Crusading group	Reason for going	Evidence from source?
Knights		
Traders, etc		

2. Now decide to what extent you think the Crusades were a holy war – a jihad. What evidence do you have to support your conclusion? What evidence is there for the opposing opinion?

How successful were the Crusades?

In Islamic history, the Crusades are given far less importance than the invasions of the Turks and Mongols. In western history, they are seen as very important events. But just how successful were they?

SUCCESS

The First Crusade captured Jerusalem in 1099 (and massacred all the Muslim men, women and children), established the Christian territories of Outremer on the coast and built some massive castles. One reason for their success was the surprise of the unprovoked Christian attack. Another was the conflict between Muslim leaders, including terrorist attacks by the **Assassins**.

WHO WERE THE ASSASSINS?

The Assassins were a breakaway Muslim group who hated Muslim leaders as much as the Christians. They had secret bases high in the mountains, from where they launched their attacks, some of them suicide missions. They were fanatically loyal to their own leader who was known as The Old Man of the Mountains. It was said that this loyalty was a result of taking the drug hashish. If their leader ordered them to leap to their death from the castle walls, they would do so.

DEFEAT

The Second Crusade (1147–49) failed to achieve anything. Even worse, the Crusader army that remained in Palestine was lured into the desert by Salah ad Din, the Muslim commander. The horses of the Christian knights started dying of thirst. Finally, the whole army suffered a devastating defeat at the Battle of Hattin in 1187. The prisoners were brought before Salah ad Din. He personally beheaded the Prince Renalt but sold the 15,000 ordinary soldiers into slavery. Salah ad Din recaptured Jerusalem in 1187, allowed pilgrimages back into the city and left Outremer alone.

TRUCE

The Third Crusade (1189–92) is the most famous because it was led jointly by Richard I (the Lionheart) of England and Philip of France. When they got to Palestine, Richard and Philip had a row and the French went home. Richard's army successfully ended the Muslim siege of the

NEW WORDS

ASSASSIN: someone who murders a leader – the word comes from the Arabic *hashishin* meaning someone who takes hashish, a form of cannabis.

TRUCE: an agreement to suspend fighting.

Arab custom says that anyone offered water should be protected. Salah ad Din gave water to the man next to Renalt to pass on so that he could still kill Renalt a few moments later.

SOURCE A

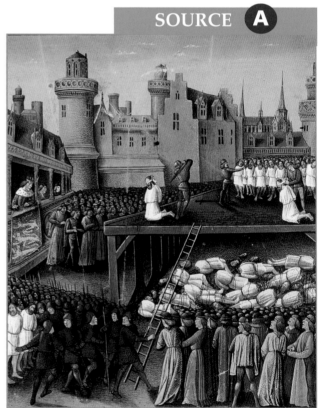

▲ *Richard Lionheart watches the execution of Muslim prisoners. Although it is a European painting, the Muslims are dressed in white suggesting their innocence.*

town of Acre. He then defeated Salah ad Din's army at the Battle of Arsuf. However, Richard knew his army was not strong enough to capture and keep Jerusalem. So he and Salah ad Din agreed a **truce** and the English king left having failed in his main objective.

LIFE IN THE OUTREMER

There were many more Crusades and in between the fighting some crusaders stayed in the Christian lands of Outremer where life was good. The weather was pleasant and they had comfortable houses rather than the cold castles and huts in Europe. There was plenty of good food and fine clothing as a result of trade through their ports. Many learned Arabic; some became spies. The Europeans were thrown out for good in 1291.

SOURCE B

There are some Franks who have settled in our country and lived among the Muslims: they are of a better sort than those who have come recently...

 Usama ibn Munquidh, warrior and writer at the time of the Crusades.

SOURCE C

The Venetians, the Genoese, and the Pisans (all Italians) are bringing choice products from the West, especially weapons and war material. This constitutes an advantage for the Muslims and an injury for the Christians.

 Salah ad Din writing to the Caliph in Baghdad.

SOURCE D

The crusaders were a nuisance rather than a serious menace. The Frankish states (Outremer) were strung out in a thin line along the coast and never included any of the great Muslim cities.

▲ *J J Saunders, 1965, A History of Medieval Islam.*

SOURCE E

Those who were poor there, has God made rich here; he who had not a village there possesses, with God as giver, a whole town here. He who was immigrant is now a resident. Why then return to the west, when the East suits us so well?

▲ *Fulcher of Chartres, medieval chronicler of First Crusade.*

Q

1. Look at **Sources B** and **C**. Describe in your own words the attitudes of Usama and Salah ad Din. How do they support the view in **Source D** that the Crusades were not that dangerous to the Islamic Empire?

2. Imagine modern TV and America were known in the Middle Ages! Write a satellite TV news report from the war zone of the first three Crusades. This could be for CNN, the American station, or for Al-Jazeera, the Arab station. Decide how you will describe:

■ Crusader success and the reasons for it
■ Muslim success and the reasons for it
■ Life in peacetime
■ The departure of the Europeans.

Two commanders compared

NEW WORDS

RANSOM: money paid to release a prisoner.
SARACENS: a medieval word for Arabs, from the Arabic work *Sarki* meaning Eastern.
SCIMITAR: a thin curved sword.

RICHARD, THE LIONHEART

Born into French royal family

Never learned English.

Became King of England after fighting his father. Known as Lionheart.

Had to keep Crusade going when the French half went home early.

Rumoured to have used the Assassins to murder a fellow Christian leader.

Captured Acre but when Salah ad Din was late paying **ransom** for the prisoners, Richard ordered all the men, women and children to be killed where the Muslim army could see.

Used a sword of hard iron for piercing armour.

Once suggested that Salah ad Din's brother should marry Richard's sister to bring peace.

Captured by Germans on way home to England. The ransom money left the whole of England poor.

SALAH AD DIN, THE UPSTART

Born in Tikrit to humble family of Kurds.

Became Vizier to the Fatimid Caliph in Cairo. Then seized power. Known as The Upstart.

Had to overcome fighting between Muslims before turning to attack Christian Crusaders.

Survived an attack in his tent by the Assassins who slashed his cheek.

After Battle of Hattin, ordered the killing of Christian prisoners by Muslim priests rather than soldiers so it would be slower and more fun to watch.

Used a **scimitar** of steel so sharp it could cut silk.

When Richard was ill, sent him fruit packed in snow to help him recover.

Famed for his generosity. When he died, Salah ad Din's treasure chest was found to have just 47 dirhams (pounds) in it.

SOURCE A

▲ *A Crusader and Saracen playing chess in an illustration from a Christian manuscript of the thirteenth century.*

SOURCE B

If Richard and Saladin could share a combination of their two characters, there would be no two princes in the world to touch them.

▲ *Bishop Herbert's reply at dinner with Salah ad Din when asked what he thought of Richard, from Norman Daniel, 1975,* **The Arabs and Medieval Europe.**

SOURCE C

The victory at Hattin owed more to the mistakes of the Franks than Salah ad Din's skill. His victories were due to his personal qualities which kept a Muslim army together longer than ever before.

▲ *Hamilton Gibb, 1973,* **The Life of Saladin.**

INVESTIGATION

Saladin and Crusader were names given to types of armoured vehicle used by the British army in the twentieth century.

You are the investigator!

Look at **Source A**. Imagine the Crusader and Saracen knights talking as they play chess. They compare what they know about Richard and Salah ad Din. Firstly, the Crusader might describe Richard's early life, followed by the Saracen about Salah ad Din; secondly, they might go on to compare their behaviour in battle; and then, thirdly, how successful they were or not. There might be some surprise at the similarities but there might also be quite an argument! Act out the conversation.

5 NEW EMPIRES FOR OLD 1500–1650

THIS CHAPTER ASKS
How did new empires emerge after the period of invasions?
What were the achievements of the Mughals?
How did two rulers survive being surrounded by threats?

NEW WORDS
SHAH: Persian word for king.
OTTOMAN: the name comes from the tribe of Othman.
JANISSARY: word meaning new troops – the special forces of the Ottoman Empire.

The invasions had been devastating but the Islamic world had absorbed them. The invaders became Muslims and everyone got used to a new ruling class whether Turkish or Mongol. From 1500, vigorous rulers created three new empires out of the old one. They had new weapons too – these were the Gunpowder Empires!

THE SAFAVID EMPIRE
In 1500, a 14-year-old youth called Ismail became leader of his religious group, the Safavid Sufis. He had great ambition and two years later he was **Shah** of a new

empire in the heart of the Islamic lands. The capital, Isfahan, was rebuilt with magnificent parks, squares, palaces and mosques.

However, Ismail turned away from the Sufi tradition. He proclaimed that the official religion would be the Shia tradition. He declared a jihad against the main Sunni tradition and ordered the execution of thousands of these fellow Muslims. To this day, Sunni and Shia Muslims are often enemies in countries such as Iraq and Iran, which were created when the Safavid Empire was broken up.

SOURCE A

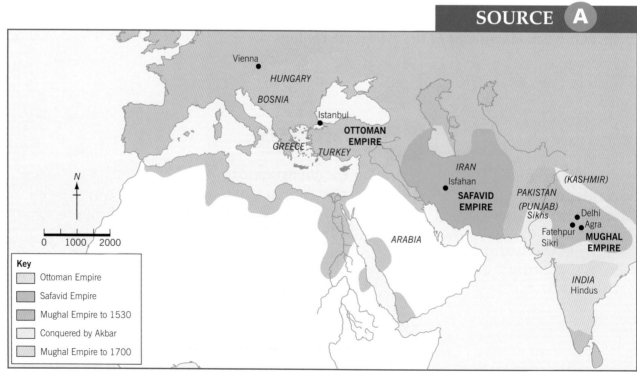

▲ *The later Islamic Empires to 1700.*

THE OTTOMAN EMPIRE

The Turks finally captured Constantinople in 1453. The city was renamed Istanbul. The Byzantine Empire collapsed and the **Ottoman** Empire rose up.

The Ottoman Empire was ruled by a Sultan. It was organised more efficiently than any previous Islamic empire. Boys between 8 and 15 from Christian villages in the empire were taken away as slaves to be trained as **Janissaries**.

However, the Ottoman Empire was also tolerant and diverse. There was official protection for Christians and Jews. In certain cities, European traders were allowed to keep their own laws. Many ideas about science and culture were exchanged with Europe. However, the religious leaders became resistant to outside ideas. For example, they got a law passed that anyone using a printing press to make copies of the Qur'an would be executed.

The most famous Sultan, Suleiman the Magnificent, pushed the boundaries of Ottoman territory further than ever. In 1529, his armies reached the gates of Vienna in the heart of Europe.

SOURCE B

Sea Voyages

1492 Italian Columbus reaches America – the start of a Spanish Empire in the New World.

1498 Portuguese Vasco da Gama, piloted by Muslim Ibn Majid, reaches India by sailing around Africa – Portuguese cities are established on the coast.

1580 Englishman Francis Drake completes the second voyage round the world – the English compete with the Spanish and Dutch for colonies around the world.

Q

1. Look at **Sources A** and **B**. What was the significance of world exploration and sea trade by Europeans for the Islamic lands?

2. Why do you think European traders were allowed their own laws in some Ottoman cities?

3. Look at **Source C**. What evidence can you see of non-Islamic influences coming back into the art?

4. Explain how the Safavid and the Ottoman Empires changed the ways in which Islamic society developed. Mention:
- relationships between Muslim groups
- relationships with non-Muslims
- achievements and influence.

SOURCE C

▲ *Safavid art embraced non-Islamic ideas.*

SOURCE D

▲ *Ottoman mosques are recognisable by their broad, low domes and tall, thin minarets.*

The Mughal Empire

The third of the new empires was created in India. Arabs had been sailing to India for trade before Islam. Muslim armies had also reached India by 750. The Sultanate of Delhi had been strong enough to keep off the Mongol invasions.

NEW WORDS

MUGHAL: a form of the word Mongol.
HINDU: follower of the main Indian religion.
GHAZI: holy warrior.

DYNASTY

The **Mughal** dynasty began in 1526 with Babur, whose family descended from the great Mongol leader Tamerlane. Babur was expelled from his family lands in the Safavid Empire. So he started raiding into India and then settled in the conquered territory. His son, Humayun, lost the Indian territory and had to go back to the Safavid Empire before regaining the lands. He died falling down some library steps after hearing the call to prayer. His death was kept secret for 17 days whilst the succession was sorted out.

SOURCE A

▲ *Mughal war elephant in full body armour reconstructed at the Royal Armouries, Leeds.*

AKBAR

Humayun's son, Jalal ud-Din, was just 14 years old when in 1556 he was proclaimed emperor to rule over nearly 150 million people, most of them **Hindus**. He turned out to be so good that he was just known as Akbar which means The Great. The Mughal Empire he established was possibly the largest ever seen and was to last for 300 years.

His army was equipped with new weapons and captured much territory across northern India including the areas now known as Punjab, Afghanistan, Pakistan and Kashmir. Akbar was less successful in conquering the south of India.

The word Mogul is now used in English about anyone powerful in business, for example, a media mogul.

SOURCE B

▲ *Mughal siege army in action.*

SOURCE C

Mughal generals erected towers of skulls from thousands of slain enemies as a terror tactic.

▲ *Stephen Dale, modern historian.*

FALLOUT AND MURDER

Akbar was succeeded peacefully by his son Jahangir. Jahangir's wife, Nur Jahan, was a real power in organising the Empire. After Jahangir's death, his sons fought each other bitterly. The winner, Shahjahan, became the next emperor. His sons couldn't wait to start fighting even before his death. The winner this time, Aurangzeb, murdered all his brothers and imprisoned his father.

Aurangzeb ruled nearly as long as Akbar did but he was the complete opposite of his ancestor. Aurangzeb was a devout Muslim and acquired the name **Ghazi**. He ended the tolerance and promotion of Hindus, reimposed special taxes on them and destroyed their temples.

Q

1. Look at **Sources A** and **B**. What evidence do they show of new developments in weapons and armour that would help a rich ruler?

2. Create a Mughal family album. Draw a portrait of each ruler in the dynasty. Underneath each picture add their name and one or two sentences about them. The rulers were:

■ Babur

■ Humayun

■ Akbar

■ Jahangir

■ Shahjahan

■ Aurangzeb.

What did the Mughals achieve?

TOLERANCE

Akbar's reign was a new golden age. He encouraged a tolerant, multi-cultural society at the eastern end of the Islamic Empires just as the same sort of society was being destroyed in Spain. He encouraged Hindus and Muslims to learn from each other's religion. Years later, the result was Sikhism, a new religion with elements of both.

BUILDING PROJECTS

Mughal emperors constructed vast palaces and gardens, including Fatehpur Sikri. Technology was developed to raise water up hundreds of metres to supply the palaces and gardens. Shahjahan was a great builder. He built a new capital near its present location, Delhi, although he called it Shahjahanabad, naturally.

THE TAJ MAHAL

Perhaps the greatest achievement was the fusion of Islamic and Hindu architectural styles that created the distinctive Mughal

domes seen at the Taj Mahal, for example. Shahjahan had the Taj Mahal built at Agra as a memorial to his beloved wife, Mumtaz Mahal, after her death. He brought together architects from many countries and 20,000 workers spent 22 years building it. The building is designed in his favourite style of white marble with lots of jewels set in the stone. The stone takes on different colours according to the time of day. Shahjahan also planned a black marble Taj but ran out of money. In fact, when the rains did not come, many people starved because Shahjahan had spent all the money on great buildings rather than irrigation and agriculture. When he was imprisoned by Aurangzeb, Shahjahan could just see the Taj Mahal in a tiny mirror in his cell.

SOURCE A

▲ *The Taj Mahal is now a World Heritage site.*

SOURCE B

درختها پی انار سه سیت کرد اکرد و حوض تمام پر کرد

جای عین باغ همین است در و قت زرد شدن پالیچه سایر

➤ *This drawing of St John was done by 12-year-old Abu'l Hasan in 1600. He was copying a well-known European drawing. He became the official palace artist of Jahangir, who loved all sorts of artistic styles.*

⋏ *Babur was not just a soldier and leader. He wrote poetry and is shown here laying out a garden. The style of Mughal gardens became world famous.*

SOURCE C

⋏ *The Mughals had several capitals. Akbar personally supervised the building of this brand new capital at Fatehpur Sikri in 1570.*

SOURCE D

Q **1.** Look at the shape of domes in **Source A** on this page and those on pages 26 and 39. Draw a diagram to show the different outlines and label them: Mughal, Ottoman, Safavid.

2. Design a poster advertising the attractions of Mughal India to European travellers in 1650. You should mention:

■ Multi-cultural tolerance

■ Art and science

■ Buildings and gardens.

Survival skills for rulers

YOUR MISSION: to prepare a 'This is Your Life' programme about two rulers surrounded by potential enemies.

Akbar's ruling class of Muslims was a tiny minority in a land of millions of Hindus. In Europe at the same time, the young queen Elizabeth had to use all her personal skills to stay queen. How did they survive?

AKBAR

Akbar was born in 1542 and reigned from 1556 to 1605.

■ *Military achievements sustained Akbar's popularity. He spent just 5% of tax income on royal palaces and 90% on forts and armies.*

■ *Akbar reduced the number of Mughals in government and increased the numbers of local Muslims and Hindus. He abolished hereditary posts and created a system of ranks and duties. Some of these were still being used in 1948. He created proper departments to record information and establish procedures fair to all.*

■ *Akbar married several Hindu princesses and allowed them to practise their religion in the palace. He allowed people to return to their own religion without fear of the death penalty. He created a building for people to learn about other religions although this wasn't popular with Muslims.*

■ *Akbar liked meeting and talking to people. He established a custom of appearing on a balcony once a day to wave to the crowds to increase his popularity. Some Muslims thought he was encouraging worship as if he was a god.*

Akbar also supported great artistic and scientific activities.
* *Many Indian and Persian **epics** were copied and illustrated.*
* *Over 100 painters were involved in the making of the book the Hamza-nama with its 1004 illustrations of legendary adventures.*
* *Many books of mathematics, science and medicine were translated and astronomical observatories were built to map the stars in the sky.*

NEW WORDS

HEREDITARY: acquired by being born into a certain family.
PROTESTANT: a member of the breakaway Church of England.
CATHOLIC: a member of the main world tradition of Christianity.

SOURCE A

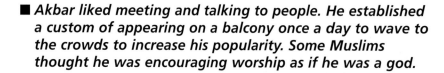

▲ *An unusually informal pencil sketch of Akbar. This again shows evidence of interest in European styles of art.*

▲ When young, Elizabeth loved parties and had many men in love with her. Later she suffered smallpox and her face was scarred. In old age she had black teeth, wore thick white makeup and a red wig.

She (Elizabeth) was an actress-producer of the royal spectacle.

▲ J M Roberts, 1996, A History of Europe.

Akbar associated with the good of every race and creed and persuasion. This was different from the practice in other realms.

▲ Jahangir, Akbar's son.

Akbar was very fond of flying pigeons, which he called 'love-making'.

ELIZABETH

Elizabeth was born in 1533 and reigned from 1558 to 1603.

■ *Elizabeth was a **Protestant** and faced threats from **Catholics** within England and abroad. She had to defeat a religious rebellion in the north of England and had 750 Catholics executed afterwards. Her ruthlessness meant that people were looking for revenge.*

■ *She never married. The kings of France and Spain were both Catholic and threatened to invade England in order to convert it back from Protestantism. Elizabeth kept off these threats by suggesting she might marry one of them or the other.*

■ *She had to order the execution of her cousin, Mary Queen of Scots, and her boyfriend, the Earl of Essex, when she found they were plotting against her.*

■ *She travelled round her country constantly. This was to show she was in control and partly because it was cheaper to stay at other people's houses!*

■ *She encouraged exploration and culture.*

Achievements in her reign were:
- *Francis Drake sailed right around the world*
- *Settlers landed in North America and named the area Virginia after her*
- *Theatres were very popular – this was the period when Shakespeare became famous.*

INVESTIGATION

You are the investigator!

Imagine you are researchers for the TV programme 'This is Your Life'. You have to prepare a script for the programme about either Akbar or Elizabeth. In the script, people who knew them will say something short about why they were a good ruler.

When you have written a script you could act it out to the rest of the class.

Index

Abbasids 11, 12, 16, 20, 30
Abd al Rahman III 12, 14, 15, 17
Abu Bakr 8
Aisha 7, 8
Akbar 40, 41, 42, 44, 45
Al Andalus 12, 13, 14, 15, 16, 17, 28, 30, 31
Al Jazeera 29, 35
Ali 8, 9
Allah 4, 22, 26
Assassins 34, 36
Astrolabe 28

Baghdad 11, 15, 21, 24, 30, 31, 35
Berber 12, 13, 16, 31
Byzantines 2, 5, 11, 31, 32, 39

Caliph 6, 8, 9, 10, 20, 30, 36, 37
Christian 2, 3, 5, 12, 13, 15, 16, 17, 30, 31, 32, 33, 35, 36, 39
Constantinople 2, 31, 39
Cordoba 14, 15, 17, 24
Crusades 31, 32, 33, 34, 35, 37

Damascus 10, 12
Dervishes 27

Elizabeth 44, 45

Fatimids 11

Hejaz 3
Hijab 22
Hindus 40, 41, 42, 44

India 3, 18, 29, 40, 43

Jerusalem 32, 34, 35
Jew(s) ~ish 3, 5, 12, 13, 17, 31, 32, 39

Khadija 4, 5, 22

Mecca 3, 4, 5, 9, 19
Medicine 28
Mongols 31, 38
Moors 13, 14, 15, 31
Mosque 19, 24
Muawiyya 8, 9
Mughals 27, 40, 41, 42, 43, 44, 45,
Muhammad 3, 4, 5, 6, 7, 8, 9, 18, 19, 23

Ottomans 39, 43

Quraish 3, 4
Qur'an 6, 7, 18, 19, 22, 26, 27, 39

Radiyya 22
Richard Lionheart 34, 36, 37

Safavids 26, 38, 40, 43
Salah ad Din 34, 36, 37
Saracen 37
Sharia 18, 22
Shias 11, 38
Sikhism 42
Slaves 16
Spain 11, 12, 13, 16, 18, 28, 42
Sufis 27, 38
Sultan 20, 22, 30, 39
Sunnis 11, 38

Turks 30, 38, 39

Umar 8
Umayyads 10, 12, 16
Uthman 6, 8

Visigoths 12, 17

Zero 28
Ziryab 15

The strange English expression So Long! is sometimes used instead of goodbye. It is thought to come from the Arabic *Salaam*! used to wish someone peace as they go away.